HUNTINGDON, ST NEOTS AND ST IVES PHOTOGRAPHIC MEMORIES

Fond Memories

Christmas 2014

Love From Ian

xxx

FRANCIS FRITH'S

HUNTINGDON,
ST NEOTS & ST IVES

PHOTOGRAPHIC MEMORIES

TOM DOIG is a social historian researching rural life in the 19th and 20th century. He is well known for his books on local history and for his radio and television programmes. During the 1980s, he held the post of Director of the Cambridge and County Folk Museum. Tom is currently running a number of lecture series for the Workers Education Association based in Cambridge as well as giving talks to local history, amenity and family history groups. He lives in a remote rural part of north Hertfordshire in a converted cattleshed built during the 1840s as part of a model farmstead. A qualified teacher and automobile engineer, he is interested in promoting history and engineering in his local primary school where he oversees a weekly engineers club. When relaxing from his history research, Tom devotes his time to the restoration of a vintage-style sports car and helping to run a Cambridgeshire motor racing team.

FRANCIS FRITH'S

PHOTOGRAPHIC MEMORIES

HUNTINGDON, ST NEOTS & ST IVES

PHOTOGRAPHIC MEMORIES

TOM DOIG

First published in the United Kingdom in 2004 by
The Francis Frith Collection

Limited Hardback Subscribers Edition Published in 2004
ISBN 1-85937-835-8

Paperback Edition 2004
ISBN 1-85937-836-6

British Library Cataloguing in Publication Data

Francis Frith's Huntingdon, St Neots & St Ives - Photographic Memories
Tom Doig

The Francis Frith Collection
Frith's Barn, Teffont,
Salisbury, Wiltshire SP3 5QP
Tel: +44 (0) 1722 716 376
Email: info@francisfrith.co.uk
www.francisfrith.com

Printed and bound in Great Britain

Front Cover: **HUNTINGDON**, *Market Hill 1929* 81874t
Frontispiece: **HUNTINGDON**, *The High Street looking East 1955*
H136003

*The colour-tinting is for illustrative purposes only, and is not intended
to be historically accurate*

AS WITH ANY HISTORICAL DATABASE THE FRITH ARCHIVE IS CONSTANTLY
BEING CORRECTED AND IMPROVED AND THE PUBLISHERS WOULD WELCOME
INFORMATION ON OMISSIONS OR INACCURACIES

CONTENTS

FRANCIS FRITH
VICTORIAN PIONEER

FRANCIS FRITH, founder of the world-famous photographic archive, was a complex and multi-talented man. A devout Quaker and a highly successful Victorian businessman, he was philosophical by nature and pioneering in outlook.

By 1855 he had already established a wholesale grocery business in Liverpool, and sold it for the astonishing sum of £200,000, which is the equivalent today of over £15,000,000. Now a very rich man, he was able to indulge his passion for travel. As a child he had pored over travel books written by early explorers, and his fancy and imagination had been stirred by family holidays to the sublime mountain regions of Wales and Scotland. 'What lands of spirit-stirring and enriching scenes and places!' he had written. He was to return to these scenes of grandeur in later years to 'recapture the thousands of vivid and tender memories', but with a different purpose. Now in his thirties, and captivated by the new science of photography, Frith set out on a series of pioneering journeys up the Nile and

to the Near East that occupied him from 1856 until 1860.

INTRIGUE AND EXPLORATION

These far-flung journeys were packed with intrigue and adventure. In his life story, written when he was sixty-three, Frith tells of being held captive by bandits, and of fighting 'an awful midnight battle to the very point of surrender with a deadly pack of hungry, wild dogs'. Wearing flowing Arab costume, Frith arrived at Akaba by camel sixty years before Lawrence of Arabia, where he encountered 'desert princes and rival sheikhs, blazing with jewel-hilted swords'.

He was the first photographer to venture beyond the sixth cataract of the Nile. Africa was still the mysterious 'Dark Continent', and Stanley and Livingstone's historic meeting was a decade into the future. The conditions for picture taking confound belief. He laboured for hours in his wicker dark-room in the sweltering heat of the desert, while the volatile chemicals fizzed dangerously in their trays. Back in London he exhibited his photographs and was 'rapturously cheered' by members of the Royal Society. His reputation as a photographer was made overnight.

VENTURE OF A LIFE-TIME

Characteristically, Frith quickly spotted the opportunity to create a new business as a specialist publisher of photographs. He lived in an era of immense and sometimes violent change.

For the poor in the early part of Victoria's reign work was exhausting and the hours long, and people had precious little free time to enjoy themselves. Most had no transport other than a cart or gig at their disposal, and rarely travelled far beyond the boundaries of their own town or village. However, by the 1870s the railways had threaded their way across the country, and Bank Holidays and half-day Saturdays had been made obligatory by Act of Parliament. All of a sudden the working man and his family were able to enjoy days out and see a little more of the world.

With typical business acumen, Francis Frith foresaw that these new tourists would enjoy having souvenirs to commemorate their days out. In 1860 he married Mary Ann Rosling and set out on a new career: his aim was to photograph every city, town and village in Britain. For the next thirty years he travelled the country by train and by pony and trap, producing fine photographs of seaside resorts and beauty spots that were keenly bought by millions of Victorians. These prints were painstakingly pasted into family albums and pored over during the dark nights of winter, rekindling precious memories of summer excursions.

THE RISE OF FRITH & CO

Frith's studio was soon supplying retail shops all over the country. To meet the demand he gathered about him a small team of photographers, and published the work of independent artist-photographers of the calibre of Roger Fenton and Francis Bedford. In order to gain some understanding of the scale of Frith's business one only has to look at the catalogue issued by Frith & Co in 1886: it runs to some 670 pages, listing not only many thousands of views of the British Isles but also many photographs of most European countries, and China, Japan, the USA and Canada - note the sample page shown on page 9 from the hand-written Frith & Co ledgers recording the pictures. By 1890 Frith had created the greatest specialist photographic publishing company in the world, with over 2,000 sales outlets - more than the combined number that Boots and WH Smith have today! The picture on the next page shows the Frith & Co display board at Ingleton in the Yorkshire Dales (left of window). Beautifully constructed with a mahogany frame and gilt inserts, it could display up to a dozen local scenes.

POSTCARD BONANZA

The ever-popular holiday postcard we know today took many years to develop. In 1870 the Post Office issued the first plain cards, with a pre-printed stamp on one face. In 1894 they allowed other publishers' cards to be sent through the mail with an attached adhesive halfpenny stamp. Demand grew rapidly, and in 1895 a new size of postcard was permitted called the court card, but there was little room for illustration. In 1899, a year after Frith's death, a new card measuring 5.5 x 3.5 inches became the standard format, but it was not until 1902 that the divided back came into being, so that the address and message could be on one face and a full-size illustration on the other. Frith & Co were in the vanguard of postcard development: Frith's sons Eustace and Cyril continued their father's monumental task, expanding the number of views offered to the public and recording more and more places in Britain, as the coasts and countryside were opened up to mass travel.

Francis Frith had died in 1898 at his villa in Cannes, his great project still growing. The archive he created continued in business for another seventy years. By 1970 it contained over a third of a million pictures showing 7,000 British towns and villages.

FRANCIS FRITH'S LEGACY

Frith's legacy to us today is of immense significance and value, for the magnificent archive of evocative photographs he created provides a unique record of change in the cities, towns and villages throughout Britain over a century and more. Frith and his fellow studio photographers revisited locations many times down the years to update their views, compiling for us an enthralling and colourful pageant of British life and character.

We are fortunate that Frith was dedicated to recording the minutiae of everyday life. For it is this sheer wealth of visual data, the painstaking chronicle of changes in dress, transport, street layouts, buildings, housing, engineering and landscape that captivates us so much today. His remarkable images offer us a powerful link with the past and with the lives of our ancestors.

THE VALUE OF THE ARCHIVE TODAY

Computers have now made it possible for Frith's many thousands of images to be accessed almost instantly. Frith's images are increasingly used as visual resources, by social historians, by researchers into genealogy and ancestry, by architects and town planners, and by teachers involved in local history projects.

In addition, the archive offers every one of us an opportunity to examine the places where we and our families have lived and worked down the years. Highly successful in Frith's own era, the archive is now, a century and more on, entering a new phase of popularity. Historians consider the Francis Frith Collection to be of prime national importance. It is the only archive of its kind remaining in private ownership. Francis Frith's archive is now housed in an historic timber barn in the beautiful village of Teffont in Wiltshire. Its founder would not recognize the archive office as it is today. In place of the many thousands of dusty boxes containing glass plate negatives and an all-pervading odour of photographic chemicals, there are now ranks of computer screens. He would be amazed to watch his images travelling round the world at unimaginable speeds through internet lines.

The archive's future is both bright and exciting. Francis Frith, with his unshakeable belief in making photographs available to the greatest number of people, would undoubtedly approve of what is being done today with his lifetime's work. His photographs depicting our shared past are now bringing pleasure and enlightenment to millions around the world a century and more after his death.

HUNTINGDON, ST NEOTS & ST IVES
AN INTRODUCTION

TO TAKE A TOUR through Huntingdonshire is like taking a walk along a river bank. At every turn, the Great Ouse and its tributaries have scoured and moulded the landscape to the south and the east, whilst the Nene has shaped the countryside to the north and the west. When Francis Frith and his successors brought their cameras to the county, they concentrated on the villages and towns strung like pearls along the banks on either side of the Great Ouse. The great towns of Huntingdon, Godmanchester, St Ives and St Neots based their prosperity on the river,

using it either as a roadway for transporting their produce or as a source of power for their developing industries. Nor should we forget the importance of the river in providing a constant supply of food - eels and fish - and also reed for basket making and thatching.

Very few of the places photographed by Frith are relatively modern. Indeed, most show evidence of settlement back to Neolithic times: the continuity of occupation is evident by their mention in the Domesday Survey of 1087. As communities have always needed a good source

ST IVES, *Market Hill c1952* S23008

10

of water, the Fen edge supplied this requirement perfectly, and our photographers hardly needed to stray from the rivers to find villages to record. Successive waves of invaders (whether by military conquest or for social reasons) used the rivers as an artery for access. The majority of movement appears to have been from east to west, although there is some north/south migration around St Neots and Eynesbury. Some of the evidence for the earliest settlements come from Neolithic deposits at Eynesbury and the southern part of St Neots. Other objects have been found at Godmanchester, Holywell and Houghton - all on higher ground, but still close to the river.

Of course it was the Romano-British period that saw the start of prosperity and an increase in population in southern Huntingdonshire. The development of Ermine Street from an Iron Age trackway into a full-blown Roman road as it sliced northwards through the county brought a new kind of civilization and improved trade. Ermine Street followed the high ground as it linked London and York, crossing the Great Ouse at Godmanchester and Huntingdon. Further north it forded the Nene at Water Newton and opened up the county from the north.

Both the forests on the high ground and the Fens on the lower ground hindered development away from the rivers and the roads, but nonetheless new trackways to the west and southeast brought trade and communication with Cambridge, along the Via Devana (now the A14), and eastwards to the communities such Ellington.

Towns such as Huntingdon and Cambridge, which had been established during the time of the Danes, evolved into the new county towns,

and by the 1500s Huntingdonshire had taken the shape that we know today.

The Civil War left its indelible mark on Huntingdonshire. Cromwell, through his family connections, enjoyed widespread support in the county, and even after the Restoration the county was a seething cauldron of unrest. Many of the larger towns lost their churches, and a number of the outlying estates saw different owners as the fortunes of the Parliamentarians and Royalists swung through success and failure.

It was the draining of the Fens that had the greatest effect on Huntingdonshire. Charles I had engaged Vermuyden, a Dutchman, to implement a grand scheme, and throughout the turmoil of the late 1600s this continued in fits and starts. The success of the plan is still with us today: the villages and towns now only experience occasional inundations rather than the former regular, seasonal floods. It has to be said, though, that when the floods come, they come with a vengeance. Few of the communities are immune, and many buildings proudly display marks indicating the level of water when the rivers burst their banks and overflow.

In the 1800s, another kind of unrest ran through the county. The Corn Laws were never accepted by the rich or the poor: for example, in June 1843 a meeting of the Anti-Corn Law League was held in Huntingdon. As well as the major landowners and townspeople, Cobden was present, and it is reported that there was a great supper for 'the high and mighty.' As in the surrounding areas, there were outbreaks of incendiarism and machine wrecking, and a number of mills and storage barns were destroyed by the rampaging mobs. The Repeal of the Corn Laws brought this to an end, and for a few years at least, matters settled down - until the beginnings of the agricultural depressions of the late 1800s.

Trade in other areas flourished, and the river, with its stone and brick wharves in the towns and wooden landing stages in the villages, was bustling with activity as the barges were loaded and unloaded. Of course, the barges were pulled by horses, and stabling, forage and farriers were needed to keep them at work. New businesses developed along the rivers - boat yards, carpentry workshops, blacksmiths, farriers, rope makers, and chandlers.

In the gazetteer covering Huntingdonshire in 1854, the entry for St Neots alone lists a whitesmith, a higgler (door to door salesman), a huckster (street salesman), a staymaker, a parchment maker, a pig dealer, a millwright, a marine store dealer, a tobacco pipe maker, a basket maker, a comb maker, a sausage maker, a letter carrier, a glover, a turner, a coach builder, a master waterman, a straw plait dealer, a machine man (stationary engine mechanic), a dyer, a scourer, an iron founder, and a currier (tanner); there were two blacksmiths, sixteen boot makers, thirteen bakers, five brewers, five maltsters, six bricklayers, fifteen carpenters, four brick makers, two millers, ten butchers, four coopers, two rope makers, two saddlers, three stonemasons, two tallow chandlers, fifteen tailors, two upholsterers, three watch and clock makers, four milliners and dressmakers, four wheelwrights, six painters, plumbers and glaziers, three printers, twenty-six innkeepers, twenty-nine beer retailers, three carriers, and two lace makers - and remember that many of these were employing a number of staff. The river had opened up new sources for supplies such as glass and bricks, whilst offering new markets for produce. Whilst the wharves, landing stages and jetties at St Neots groaned under the weight of the trade and the traders themselves, we should not forget that the town was slightly less populous than Huntingdon and Godmanchester, which were just as busy. To all this activity we must

ST NEOTS, *Brierley's Landing Stage c1955* S37022

add that of the villages along the riverside. Huntingdonshire was beginning to find itself in trade; like Cambridge, it was open to Kings Lynn, and looking to international commerce with the continent and the Baltic.

And what of the people? What were they like? In 1794, the Honourable John Byng wrote in his Torrington Diaries about a journey from St Neots to Cambridge. He describes leaving St Neots on the road southwards, 'thru a vile dreary country with nothing to see or amuse. I came to the village of Eltisley, a place as deplorable as I hope to see unmatched in Britain. Are we fighting for the wrong of France, are we to preserve Holland, are we to think of nothing but trade, and to brag of our numerous ships, when our land is desolate, our poor oppressed, the interior of our country threadbare, to finance a tinsel fringe, an exterior of Trade, that bane of comfort, that selfish unfeeling monster? To two human male beings, whose nakedness was not concealed by rags, who held my horse, I gave my loose halfpence. Never had they known such treasure. Covering for head and feet they had never known. They seem to be about 12 or 14 years of age.' Either things were very bad at Eltisley, or the entrepreneurial spirit of the young lads of the town successfully fleeced Byng of his 'loose halfpence' - I would like to think the latter.

Many of the townspeople prospered and fine residences were built in the high streets. The parish churches were renovated and embellished. Non-conformity moved from strength to strength, and where other counties saw the building of chapels and missions rooms, the towns in Huntingdonshire had proper non-conformist churches. The people lived by their wits - it is particularly heartening to note that the Barley Mow at Hartford was built from the second-hand stones left over from the spire of St Benedict's Church at Huntingdon, an example of true re-cycling two hundred years ago.

The people from the Fens and the Fen edge have a reputation for being slow-witted, dour and dismissive - but nothing could be further from the truth. It is true that their language might seem a little odd - who would have thought to pronounce Houghton 'Hoe-tun' and Whyton 'Whitton'? But who am I, a Scotsman from Auld Reekie, to criticize? During my research for this book my wife and I have been greeted with friendliness and courtesy. The best way that I can thank all those that we met is to echo the words of King James I (and VI of Scotland) when he thanked Sir Oliver Cromwell, grandfather of the Lord Protector, after visiting Hinchingbrook: 'Marry man, thou has treated me better than anyone since I left Edinborg.'

HUNTINGDON, ST NEOTS AND ST IVES

▶ **EATON SOCON**
The Parish Church of St Mary the Virgin 1897
39997

The parish church of St Mary the Virgin appears to have been built in the early 15th century using some earlier parts, which possibly date from the 14th century. Unfortunately, in February 1930 the church was destroyed by fire, and only the west tower and the vestry survived. Rebuilding was immediately put in hand, and the restored church was re-consecrated in 1932.

EATON SOCON, *The White Horse, the Great North Road c1960* E202012

The White Horse dates back to the 13th century, and was later a Royal Mail staging post. Charles Dickens mentions the house in *Nicholas Nickleby*. It is believed that during the heyday of the trade thirty six coaches passed each day to and from London along the Great North Road through the village. The community was of great importance to travelers: many of the buildings provided rest and accommodation, whilst other housed service trades such as wheelwrights, leather workers and blacksmiths.

EATON SOCON, *The Green and the Memorial c1960* E202015

Easton Socon was originally in Bedfordshire, 'on the borders of Huntingdonshire'; the early 20th-century directories tell us that the parish covered over 7000 acres, but only had a population of 2000. In 1965, the county boundaries changed and Eaton Socon, with Eaton Ford, became part of Huntingdonshire. Less than ten years later, Huntingdonshire was merged with Cambridgeshire, and the residents could truthfully say that they were amongst the few that had lived in the same house but in three counties in fewer than ten years.

EYNESBURY
St Mary Street 1897
39994

We are looking northwards along St Mary Street, and the tower of St Neots parish church dominates the skyline. Eynesbury is separated from St Neots by the Hen Brook, which was bridged as early as 1540. Indeed, it could be argued that St Neots forms a part of Eynesbury, as the community here predates St Neots by a thousand or so years, having been formed during the Bronze Age. Many of the houses in the photograph are still recognisable today, although the barber's shop offering 'hair cutting and shaving' on the left is now a private house. Today the traffic weaves between parked cars; in 1897 only a delivery cart and a drop-handled sports bicycle are visible.

EYNESBURY, *St Mary Street c1965* E216050

Almost exactly the same view as No 39994 (pages 16-17) shows
that little has changed: even the bicycle, albeit a little more
modern in design, seems to form the main method of transport.
A shopping precinct has replaced the building in the right
foreground. On the right, Knowles bakery has become a Chinese
take-away, and the nearest foreground building is occupied
by the St Neots Motor Cycle Company. The fish and chip shop
sporting the Walls ice-cream sign (beyond the bakery) and today
occupied by St Neots Picture Gallery was the home of the Tebbutt
family, who were well known champion Fen ice skaters.

EYNESBURY
The Parish Church of St Mary the Virgin 1897 39995

A church is mentioned here at Eynesbury in the Domesday survey, but today no evidence of this is visible on the ground, of course. The earliest parts of the present church date from the late 12th century. A tower appears to have been added in the late 1200s, when both aisles were built. In 1685, the tower collapsed and destroyed the chancel, the south aisle and most of the nave. The chancel and tower were rebuilt in 1687. It is said that the work on the chancel was poorly executed; nearly 200 years later, in 1858, it was totally rebuilt.

EYNESBURY, *Conygear Mills 1897* 39992

This is the River Mill, Eaton Socon (rear view), two miles away from Conygear Mills. Formerley a flower mill owned by Jordan Addington's grain merchants. Later used for fitting out narrow boats and currently a pub and restaurant.

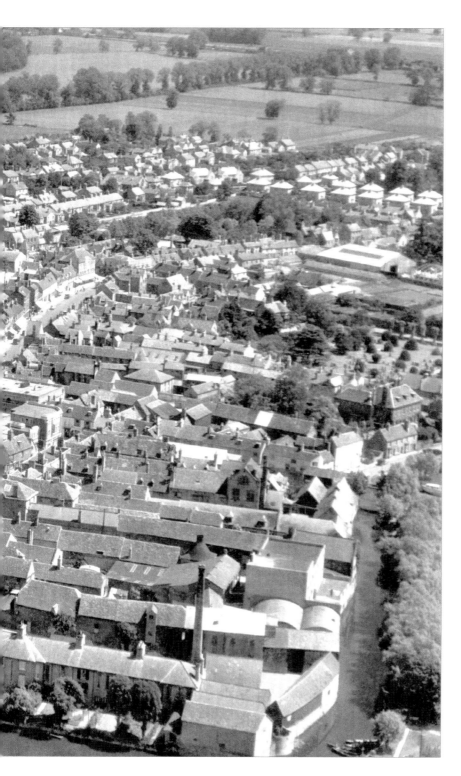

ST NEOTS
From the Air c1955
S37013

The ancient bridge in the foreground - the site dates from before 1180 - was in 1964 found to be unsafe and replaced. In around 1910 the Public Rooms on the south of the bridge had been used as a roller skating rink and a few years later as a cinema. By the late 1950s it was redundant, and was sold to St Neots UDC, who demolished it in 1963 to make way for a temporary bridge during the rebuilding of the St Neots Bridge. A bus is parked outside the Cross Keys, maybe delivering passengers from the railway station - the inn advertised 'meeting every train' in the mid 19th century when the coaching business slipped into a decline. The west and south sides of the town are bounded by the River Ouse and the Hen Brook. The course of the High Street and the Market Square are clearly visible. In the centre of the view, the spire of the Congregational church stands out proudly.

▶ **ST NEOTS**
*Brierley's Landing
Stage c1955* S37022

Brierley's hired out rowing boats, canoes and punts from their landing stage at the corner of the Ouse and Hen Brook. Their garden and tea-rooms were a popular meeting place for the young people of the town and for visitors. In 1895, St Neots announced the opening of its spa of refreshing and invigorating water emanating from a spring by the Paper Mill. 'Neotia', as the red-coloured water was called, was so foul-tasting that very few people bought it, and the venture failed. Mr Brierley, however, made a small fortune on the spa's first day by providing, at a modest charge, suitably decorated river craft to form a procession along the River Ouse.

◀ **ST NEOTS**
*River Terrace and the Ouse
c1955* S37006

During the floods of 1947, the River Ouse rose over the gardens of the twelve houses in River Terrace and drenched the ground floors. By 1955, everything appears to have settled down, and pleasure craft and punts are using the boat yards, landing stages, riverside cafes and the garden to the Old Falcon Inn (left). Even Brierley's boatyard on the corner of the Hen Brook (right) is back in business. During the 1990s, River Terrace was demolished, and a new complex of houses and flats fills the area between the River and Brook Street.

ST NEOTS, *Brook Street c1955* S37008

Next to the Bushel & Strike public house (left), in what was the Bell Yard, stands Ibbett's blacksmith and engineering workshop's outside store. The business goes back to the 17th century, and was started by the landlord of the Bell, who was also a blacksmith. John Duke held the Bell and the business, but after his death in 1851, it was sold to Thomas Ibbett. The business continued through the 1800s and into the 1900s in the same family. The yard had been a building which was demolished around 1915. The house next door became Ibbett's office after the closure of the White Swan in the 1920s. Opposite the Bushel & Strike, the gap in the wall originally opened onto a set of steps leading down to the landing stage on the Hen Brook.

◄ **ST NEOTS**
The Bridge and the Bridge Hotel c1955 S37011

In 1964 this beautiful and historic bridge, built in 1617, finally bent to the increase of traffic and was demolished and replaced with a modern concrete structure. Apart from the need for something stronger, it was believed that the small arches restricted the flow of the Ouse and led to the formation of ice during the winter. At the same time as the rebuilding, the osier beds on the northern side were taken up and Riverside Park was created. The white building is the Bridge Hotel, whilst on the south side are the Public Rooms, opened in 1855 to provide a place for public meetings and concerts.

ST NEOTS
The Market Square c1965
S37034

On this busy day, all of the parking spaces in the Market Square have been taken. As well as the ubiquitous Minis and Morris Minors, we can see a rare Y type MG saloon, a Jaguar Mk 7, a Chevrolet Impala station wagon and a Vauxhall FB Victor estate car. By the time of the photograph, many of the well-known High Street stores had set up branches in the town, including Boots the 'Cash Chemist' (left), F W Woolworth (centre right) and Freeman, Hardy & Willis. None the less, the enduring St Neots traders still have a foothold, and R E Cadge, outfitters (centre), and W Eayres, butcher, are open for business.

ST NEOTS, *The Market Square c1965* S37032

The photographer has turned his camera a little to the south and included an additional couple of interesting cars - a Rover 90 and behind it a rare and expensive Bristol saloon. The range of premises on the right are the offices and entrance to Paine's brewery. In 1814 the business was bought by John Day, and during 1822 he had the cast iron memorial erected in the market square. Standing on a stone base, the lantern was originally powered by oil, but it was later changed to gas.

ST NEOTS
The High Street 1897 39975

The motor-car had not arrived by the sixtieth year of Queen Victoria's reign, and yet the High Street still seems familiar. The corner pillar and the cast iron railings of the Congregational Church (right) are still pristine after their installation in 1888. The National Westminster Bank has not yet arrived, and the premises next door are occupied by Ellwoods. Beyond, under the awning (now Martins the newsagent's) is Buxton's paper shop, and further on stands the Three Tuns public house. On the opposite side, just west of the Dewdrop Inn, works one of those forgotten craftsmen who were once a familiar sight in our towns and villages, the knife and razor sharpener. He has parked his chain-driven grindstone and is preparing to hone a pair of scissors or maybe a kitchen knife.

ST NEOTS
The High Street 1925
77204

The Westminster Bank (right) has taken over from Ellwoods, and the trees have begun to grow in the front yard to the Congregational Church. In the distance, the columned lantern on the Pavilion Cinema, the old Corn Exchange, is silhouetted against the skyline. In fewer than five year it will be gone forever in a terrible fire. On the south side, whilst a touring charabanc waits for its customers outside the Royal Oak public house, a handcart makes a delivery to Fraser's, piano sellers and household outfitters.

27

ST NEOTS
The High Street c1955 S37007

On 1 January 1870, John Lynn, ironmonger, took the third premises down on the right. He fought a long and bitter war with the Local Board demanding the right of shopkeepers to display their goods on the pavement in front of their shops. He failed, and was convicted and fined 6d. On John's death in 1911, his son, Howard, took over; from this view, he appears not to have been deterred by the decision of the Board. The shop continued under the Lynn family until Howard died in 1964. Through the arch under Riseleys, ladies' fashions(to the right of Lynn's), was the yard of Edward 'Teddy' Ireland, the manufacturer of the engine and chassis for the Vulcan motor car. He later took the agency for Panhard, Star, Darraq, Renault and de Dion cars. The premises later became offices and showrooms for the Gas Board. Riseleys is spanned by Ibetts, fruit and vegetables, and Femina, a ladies' hairdresser. On the opposite side of the road stands Lloyds Bank and the Three Tuns public house.

ST NEOTS
Huntingdon Street c1955
S37004

We are at the junction of Huntingdon Street and the High Street, and on the north-east corner of The Cross is a rather bland building (right). This was the home of the Bellingham family. On 11 May 1812, John Bellingham, suffering under what he felt was a grievance towards the Government, entered the House of Commons where he shot and killed the Prime Minister, Mr Spencer Percival. This was the first time that a Prime Minister had been assassinated, and vengeance was swift. Bellingham was hanged within the week. The house later became a solicitor's office, and is now an 'Open Door' church.

ST NEOTS, *The High Street from The Cross c1965* S37070

The Cross, the junction of the High Street, Cambridge Street, Huntingdon Street and Church Street, marks the original site of the centre of town, and was a planned medieval market place. It is first mentioned during the early 15th century. The spire of the Congregational church stands proudly above the row of shops spanned by the Westminster Bank and the premises of John Rayns Smith (the first white building on the right). The church, whose foundation stone was laid on 19 June 1888 by Joseph Wilcox, was built to replace the Old Meeting House of 1715. Unfortunately, the Meeting House was destroyed by fire in the late 1960s. The Congregational church has now become St Neot's United Reformed Church.

ST NEOTS
The High Street 1925
77213

The Pavilion cinema on the right was originally built in 1863 as the Corn Exchange. During the 1890s, it was used as a museum; later, in 1915, it was converted into a cinema. In 1929, a fire reduced it to a smouldering ruin. The interior was rebuilt, and the exterior, apart from the towered and domed lantern which was lost, was renovated. The Pavilion closed in 1968, and the building was demolished in 1978. Around the same time, the bracketed clock disappeared; it had been erected by a public subscription of £64 to commemorate Queen Victoria's Jubilee in 1887. On the opposite corner is Freeman, Hardy & Willis's shoe shop (now the Edinburgh Wool Shop), and further down is the International Tea Company.

▶ **ST NEOTS**
*The Market Square and
High Street c1955* S37001

The roof line of the buildings
facing onto the north side of
the Market Square shows little
change today. However, although
the Cross Keys (left) remains,
many of the names above the
shops have changed. Here we see
the Priory sweet shop and café
next to the Cross Keys, and then
Boots (on the site of Wrights); W
Eayres, butcher and member of
the town's bellfounding family
(the business started around
1911 on site previously held by
Matthews, and later in 1958 was
totally rebuilt; R E Cadge, men's
clothier; a straw plait and hat
dealer; then F W Woolworth,
previously the Angel Inn, where
human skeletons were found
during renovations. But even the
Cross Keys changed, albeit in a
very small way - a couple of years
earlier, it switched its allegiance
from the AA to the RAC!

◀ **ST NEOTS**
The High Street c1955 S37020

An Austin Twelve is parked outside
the Westminster Bank (right),
which still sports the flagpole
erected as part of the 1953
Coronation celebrations. On this
sunny day, there is so little moving
traffic that the lady just beyond
the bank is able to push her
mother in a wheelchair across the
road without impunity towards
the Royal Oak public house. Only
the Austin stands on the north
side of the High Street, whilst the
only gap in the parked cars on the
south side is between the Standard
8 and the Riley. Maybe there was
some unrecorded parking code?

▲ **ST NEOTS,** *The High Street c1960* S37028

On the north side of the High Street, behind the Mini Traveller stands the Westminster Bank, previously Ellwoods; next door is R & O Hall, newsagents, who later became Buxton's paper shop and is now a branch of Martins. Then comes the premises of Dudeney & Johnston, who were originally located on the Market Square. After them is Plum's restaurant and the Three Tuns public house. The names of the shops may have changed today, but the roof line is still recognisable.

◄ **ST NEOTS**
Roper's Shop, Cambridge Street c1968
S37060

Roper's shop started life as a baker's, but by 1968 it was stocking all kinds of attractive goods. Jars of sweets line the shelves, chocolate bars are displayed on the counter for impulse buying, the refrigerator is full of ice-creams and the glass case in front of the shop assistant overflows with cosmetics and household products. The aerosol cans of deodorant must be among the first to come into use, although disinfectant is still being sold in glass bottles. Many of the goods, including the Parkinson's sweets, would have been carefully weighed on the Avery scales by the immaculately coiffeured lady assistant. Children would have opened their purchases and dropped the wrappers into the waste bin (centre) provided under a token scheme run by Fairy Soap. Today, Roper's has been split into two premises - Unwin's off-licence and an American Burger Bar.

33

▼ **GREAT STAUGHTON,** *St Andrew's Church c1955* G279009

Saint Andrew's Church, at the north of the village and on the Causeway, was reported in 1636 to be 'much ruinated', and major repairs were necessary. Later, between 1848 and 1850, extensive maintenance was undertaken, but it was not up to the required standard - the church was totally rebuilt in 1866. The tower bears an important plaque warning bell ringers from practising during thunderstorms. Next door to the church stood the Robin Hood and Little John public house. This was de-licensed in 1948, and is now home to the Taggert Gallery and Tile Museum.

▶ **GREAT STAUGHTON**
The Highway c1955 G279004

Opposite Odell's garage (right) lies the non-conformist chapel, now an immaculate private residence. The foundation stone was laid by Bateman Brown on 15 August 1871. Typical of its time, the yellow brick building is decorated with bands of red, yellow and black terracotta tiles. The frontage of Mumford's Stores (left), once the post office, was rebuilt in 2004, but its character survives. Odell's garage started as a workshop for the repair of agricultural equipment, but with the arrival of motor transport, it quickly became a garage and service station. It remains with the same family of Odell today.

GREAT STAUGHTON
The Sundial c1955
G279006

Standing in front of a shop (now a private residence called Dial House), the sundial has been a prominent feature of Great Staughton since 1637. It stands on a pyramid-shaped brick plinth surmounted by a carved stone pillar, and the hour can be read using the cast iron gnomon. Further back, on the left is the butcher's shop of G M Gilbert, and then the White Hart public house. On the deceptively quiet Highway, the van makes its delivery to Odell's garage.

ELLINGTON
The Parish Church of All Saints' 1906 55437

A church at Ellington is mentioned in the Domesday survey of 1086. The chancel arch of the present church dates from the 13th century, and the tower was added in around 1390. Shortly afterwards, the nave arcades, north aisle and the north porch, shown in the photograph, were added. During the 1860s, Sir George Gilbert Scott redesigned and rebuilt the chancel. This view shows the church after the restoration of the spire in 1899 but before the rebuilding of the nave roof in 1907.

ELLINGTON
The Village 1906 55436

Ellington lies on the present A14 road to the west of Huntingdon. At Domesday, the manor was held by the Abbot of St Benedict's, Ramsey, and the parish had a population of about 150. By 1906, when the photograph was taken, the population had risen to around 260. The farmer in his trap and the pair of roadmen appear to be the only inhabitants - but of course most people would be working in the fields preparing the land for the coming winter.

37

▼ **ST NEOTS,** *The Paper Mill at Little Paxton 1897* 39988

The paper mill was built on the site of a corn mill called Okestubbe Mill, which was owned by St Neots Priory and continued to operate until the early 19th century. In 1799, the mill was bought by Ousley Rowley, a local landowner, who let it to a Mr Hobson of Eaton Socon. Shortly afterwards it was taken over by Henry Fourdrinier, one of the most innovative of local paper makers, but the cost of development broke him, and by 1808 he was bankrupt. Eventually, after a chequered career, the mill became the St Neots Paper Mill, owned by George Fydell Rowley; it employed over 200 people. In 1912, a disastrous fire destroyed the building in the photograph, but a new, state-of-the art paper mill was built the following year and the business continued to thrive.

▶ **OFFORD DARCY**
The Village 1906 55441

Offord Darcy stands on the main road between St Neots and Huntingdon. On the bend at the centre of the village is the Horse Shoe public house (left), which survives and thrives today. Beside it is Rectory Farm House, now almost obscured by trees; the thatched barn next door has been demolished, a victim to the need to straighten the bend. The building on the right is now occupied by Offord Motor Company.

◀ **OFFORD CLUNY**
The Village 1906
55438

A builder balances on a plank across two ladders (centre right) to carry out a meticulous repair to the stone balls on the gate to the Manor. So successful was his work that the balls survive today. On the other side of the road, at the junction to Station Road, a farmer's trap waits for the Swan public house to open. Little has changed at this junction; even the wrought iron railings on the left have avoided various wartime scrap iron drives and are still in place. Station Road, on the left, leads over the railway and across the Great Ouse to the mill.

▶ **OFFORD CLUNY**
The Mill 1906 55439

Along Station Lane, westwards out of Offord Cluny, the mill is silhouetted against the skyline. We are looking across the complex of locks and weirs on the Great Ouse, and little has changed today. The chimney has been demolished, and during the past few years the mill has been renovated and restored by Campbell Melhuish. Today it comprises blocks of executive apartments overlooking the pleasure craft moored in Buckden Marina. However, surviving almost unchanged are the Mill House and on the right Mill Cottage, built in 1851.

▶ **HILTON**
Grove End c1955
H440014

This row of terraced labourers' cottages lies opposite Hilton Village Hall, previously the school, and adjacent to the maze. On the left is Douglas Cottage, then the plainly named No 2, and the last house on the right is Green Cottage. Since the photograph was taken, there has been some rebuilding to the house on the right behind the fine razor-edged Triumph Renown motor-car, and a garage has been constructed at Douglas Cottage. But apart from a few new trees, little else has changed.

◀ **HILTON**
The Unicursal Maze c1955
H440029

Close to the cottages at Grove End, the beautifully maintained maze commemorates the restoration of King Charles II to the throne. The Latin on the memorial reads: 'William Sparrow, gentleman, born in the year 1641, aged 88 when he died, fashioned this circle in the year 1660.' One of only eight mazes surviving in Britain, it is of the unicursal type - there are no dead ends, and the narrow grass track leads circuitously to the centre without any deviation. It is said that the Hilton Maze is based on the design of the lost maze at Comberton, where Sparrow's brother-in-law Barron Brittain lived.

▲ **FENSTANTON,** *Chequer Street c1955* F191003

We are looking along Chequer Street towards Honey Hill; the shape of the community has changed little. The Chequers pub (centre right) is now a private house; the next building has been demolished, but Chequers House, in the foreground, has been restored, and today sports fine wrought iron railings and a splendid iron gate arch. The Rover 90 is parked outside a row of late 19th-century terraced cottages. These have been replaced by a row of similar, but modern, terraced houses. The large traffic island (centre) today splits a one-way system, and in the spring is a delight of yellow daffodils.

◄ **FENSTANTON**
The Parish Church of St Peter and St Paul 1898 41299

The landscape designer Lancelot 'Capability' Brown is buried here at Fenstanton with his wife and children. He bought the manor of Fenstanton in 1768 for £13,000. Brown would have been proud of the pollarded walkway through the churchyard, which even today is perfectly maintained. A bell was given to the church in 1981 by the John Howland Society of America: at the time of religious intolerance, Howland emigrated from Fenstanton to America aboard the *Mayflower* in 1620. The fine spire dominates the skyline and announces Fenstanton across the low-lying Fenland.

◄ **SWAVESEY**
The High Street c1965 S675019

The quiet High Street, populated only by a Ford 105E Anglia, a Wolseley Hornet, a Ford Consul, and (peeping out of the corner on the left) a Fordson tractor, is a far cry from the days when Swavesey enjoyed its annual and weekly markets. On 26th July 1244, Alan la Zouche and his heirs were granted a Tuesday market and a yearly three-day market at the Feast of Holy Trinity. The market day changed over the years, and it finally closed around 1890. Today, however, the High Street is again a busy thoroughfare taking traffic between the villages and Cambridge.

◄ **SWAVESEY**
The Cobblestones
c1965 S675009

In 1827 the village of Swavesey bought a second-hand fire engine from Merryweathers of London. It was still in use in 1913, when the village suffered a disastrous fire which destroyed the whole row of cottages, apart from the house bearing the 'Sold' sign (second from the right). In total the homes of twenty-two families comprising sixty-three people were lost. Of the new houses in the photograph, the village history records: 'the world of thatch cottages and horse-drawn pumps was giving way to slate and bricks and motors.'

▲ **SWAVESEY,** *The Parish and Priory Church of St Andrew 1898* 41295

During the religious turmoil of the 1600s, the registers at Swavesey record some unusual goings-on. In 1626, Thomas Christian and Elizabeth Rooke were married by one William Batter, 'who reads prayers one day at Swavesey and another at Over and his father preacheth accordinglie and serves cure at Swavesey for one time as his sonne doth at another and neither of them is licenses; neither is the son in orders.' One speculates as to the legitimacy of Thomas and Elizabeth's children.

◄ **OVER**
The Parish Church
c1965 O114004

We are looking down Station Street towards the church. On the left are Walnut Bake House and Albion Villa, whilst in the right foreground is Gilbert's Cottage. This cottage had now been rebuilt and extended. Little else has changed over the past forty years, although today the busy corner where the road sweeps to the right into Church End is a major hazard to traffic.

OVER, *The Mill c1965* O114010

The Domesday survey does not mention a mill at Over. Even if it did, the mill would have been a watermill, as windmills did not appear in England until the mid 1100s. Up to the end of the 1800s, windmills were a familiar sight across the Fens. This example at Over is a tower mill with a rotating cap. The fantail would have rotated the cap to make sure that the sails faced into the wind. Here, at Over, the mill was employed in grinding corn; it should not be confused with many others that were, in essence, used for pumping the drains and dykes.

EARITH
The High Street c1955
E201018

Earith is situated on the northern bank of the Great Ouse at its junction with the Old West River and the Old and New Bedford Rivers. When the Fens are frozen, the ice-covered lowlands around the town are popular with fen skaters. If the ice is of the highest quality, Earith is the venue for the English National Skating Championships. On the right, in the distance, stands the Crown Inn. During the middle ages, feudal rights and issues were settled at the Manor Court held here.

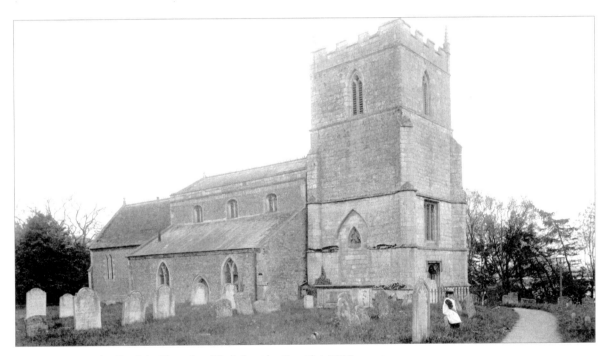

HOLYWELL, *The Parish Church of St John the Baptist 1898* 41298

The church of St John the Baptist was built in the Early English style. Amongst its rectors was Thomas Tenison (1667-81), who became Archbishop of Canterbury in 1696. The village takes it name from the ancient spring whose stone canopy, built in 1845, can still be seen on the slope to the south of the church. This has recently been restored and will continue to be 'dressed' each June during the Patronal festival. In the photograph, a young girl sits on the footstone to what appears to be the grave of John Luill, who died in 1748. The years have taken their toll on the carving, and today the lettering is almost indecipherable.

HOLYWELL
The Great Ouse 1914
66968

Holywell developed by the Great Ouse as a traditional 'ring' village: the main street runs around the perimeter of the community with only one access road. In the photograph, Tom Metcalfe oversees one of the men, who is about to use his punt to collect osiers and reeds. In the background on the left stands Brooklyn; then, with two thatched eyebrow gables, comes Anchor Cottage, previously the Anchor public house. On the right, with the three bay windows, is Reed Cottage, the winner of a recent 'Best Cottage' award. This was the home of the Fraser family of artists, whose work was exhibited at the Royal Academy. Garden William Fraser (1856-1921), who worked under the name of W F Garden, and Arthur Anderson Fraser were members of the White Cockade Club and the Legitimist Jacobite League of Great Britain and Ireland, which hoped to depose Queen Victoria and reinstate the Stuart dynasty.

▼ **HOLYWELL,** *The Ferry Boat Inn c1960* H407060

At the extreme end of the 'ring' is the Ferry Boat Inn. The Ferry Boat claims to be one of the oldest inns in Britain. A ferry crossed the river close to the Ferry Boat for many years, and it is reputed that Hereward the Wake used it to escape from the Normans. Each year on 17 March the ghost of Juliet Tewsley appears at the Ferry Boat as she re-enacts her lovelorn suicide of 1050. Today, the river traffic has declined, and the Ferry Boat, once busy with waterborne customers, is a popular place for evening refreshments with the people of St Ives and the surrounding villages.

► **HEMINGFORD ABBOTS**
St Margaret of Antioch Church from the River 1899 44253

This photograph looks across the Ouse from a spot close to Battcock's Island. The impressive spire of St Margaret's Church is outlined against the skyline; it survived a massive lightning strike in 1862. Ten years later, the church was extensively restored, and in 1911 it was partly rebuilt. The Ouse is the venue for the annual Regatta - only the war years have seen it cancelled. The original Vicar's Sculls trophy was first presented in 1904 by the Rev Byrom Holland. A silver plaque set into the wall between the churchyard and the river marks the starting place for the races. The church is famous for its biannual flower festival which draws enthusiasts from all over the country.

◀ HEMINGFORD ABBOTS
Common Lane 1914 66964

It is sometimes almost unbelievable when we realise how much of our heritage has been destroyed during the past century. This beautiful house would seem to be such an important asset to the village, but like so many others, all trace of it has now gone. In its place stands a row of brick terraced cottages. In the distance, the thatched building with the brick chimney forms part of the original village school and the School House. We may be thankful that this survives and is being meticulously cared for by its present owner.

▶ HEMINGFORD ABBOTS
The Village c1955 H159044

One of the first buildings that the visitor will meet is the picturesque 15th-century thatched Axe and Compasses public house (centre). A family-run business, the Axe and Compasses is situated in the hub of the village and village life. Hemingford Abbots no longer has a village shop, and in part the pub carries out this function by selling stamps and other items. On the right of the tree, the low tiled building is the Forge (now Forge Cottage), whilst the brick-fronted houses are the delightfully named April and May Cottages.

49

▶ **HEMINGFORD GREY**
St James' Church and the Great Ouse 1898 41288

The church of St James at Hemingford Grey comprises a chancel, a vestry, north and south aisles, a nave, a tower and a south porch. In 1741, the spire was blown off in a great gale. The stump was leveled off and the spire was never replaced. A major restoration was carried out in 1859 at a cost, found by public subscription, of £1200. Inside the door to the south porch stands a fine early medieval octagonal font, whilst opposite this, against the north wall, a superb organ by Bryceson Bros of Highbury provided accompaniment to the voices of the congregation. The gentle Great Ouse not only formed the northern boundary of the village, but it was a main source of trade and communication with Huntingdon and St Ives. Today it is used by pleasure craft.

◀ **HEMINGFORD GREY**
The Manor c1955 H408003

Built around 1130, the Manor is supposed to be the oldest continuously inhabited house in Britain. Lucy Maria Wood Boston, born in December 1892, bought the building in 1939 and spent two years restoring it. During the Second World War she kept open house for the RAF officers stationed at the nearby airfield at Wyton, and arranged musical and literary evenings. She used the Manor as an inspiration for her series of six children's stories known as the Green Knowe books. The house is open to the public by appointment.

▲ **HEMINGFORD GREY,** *The Apex c1955* H408013

The Apex stands in the fork of the junction between the High Street and Church Street, both of which lead down to old landing stages on the Great Ouse. Today, little has changed. The pavement in front of the Apex has been kerbed, and the house has had new and more traditional windows installed. The front door has been painted a buttercup yellow and a garage has been added on the right. The telephone kiosk peeping into the frame on the right still stands, and Number 22 High Street on the left has been restored and repainted, and sports a beautiful 'Welcome' plaque on its door frame.

◄ **HEMINGFORD GREY**
The High Street c1955
H408035

We are looking eastwards towards the Apex along the High Street. The Cock public house (left) stands at the corner of Church Lane opposite Braggs Lane. The Cock is now a particularly fine restaurant, and has been awarded recognition by Les Routiers. The black wooden shed beyond has been demolished to make way for a car park. The general stores next door is now the Willow Guest House, whilst the dwelling next door again has been renamed The Old Post Office. The last white building is the Jubilee Reading Room and St James Parish Centre.

► ST IVES
The Bridge 1899 44244

The first recorded wooden bridge was built here on the site of the original ford in the early 12th century. The present bridge was constructed in Barnack stone in 1414, and the chapel of St Ledger (or St Lawrence as some records suggest) was consecrated in 1426. In 1645, during the Civil War, one arch was removed and replaced with a drawbridge. The drawbridge was demolished and the round-headed arches were rebuilt in 1716. Two extra stories were added to the chapel in 1836 and it became a private house, but in 1930 the structure was found to be unstable, and the chapel was returned to its original design.

◄ **ST IVES**
The Quay c1960 S23079

In the 17th and 18th centuries, the Quay was a scene of bustling activity with barges loading and unloading their cargoes. The buildings in the main date from the 18th century, and were constructed to meet the needs (and provide refreshment for) the river workers. Today, the waterborne traffic is mainly pleasure craft, and the Quay is a favourite place for children to feed the ducks and for visitors to relax and absorb the pleasant view. Photographed from an upper storey of the 1854 steam mill, now converted to flats, the buildings are reflected in the still water of the Ouse. Today they range from business management services and marketing consultants, antiques shops, and cafes to private homes. On the right is a boatyard. One of the town's famous oarsmen was John Goldie, the son of the vicar. He was three times stroke for Cambridge in the Boat Race boat, and gave his name to the University's second boat.

ST IVES, *Bridge Street 1898* 41280

ST IVES, *Bridge Street 1955* S23004

Today, the bridge at St Ives is restricted to pedestrians, but up to fifty years ago, it was possible to drive a cart or a car over the bridge. On the left in the 1955 view is the Manor House, occupied by Wadsworth, the beer and soft drink bottlers, whilst on the right is the building which used to be the Temperance Hotel. The 1898 view shows the earlier type of blinds used by the shops to protect their goods: the awning is supported on wooden posts driven into the road surface. Whilst a Jaguar 2½ litre heads a row of cars in 1955, only a little boy with a pram uses the road in 1898. At the far end, facing across Bridge Street, is the old Crown Inn with its distinguishing cross on the upper panel. It was demolished after a fire in 1975 and rebuilt for Woolworth's in a sympathetic manner.

ST IVES
*The Parish Church of All Saints',
the Interior 1898* 41285

ST IVES
The Parish Church of All Saints' 1899
44251

Nothing serves better than to quote the town guide provided by the impressive Norris Museum: 'This church marks the site of the Saxon village of Slepe, the original centre of settlement before St Ivo's Priory was built. Most of the present building dates from the late 15th century and there is a 13th-century archway in the north side of the chancel. Interesting fittings include a 13th-century font, an Elizabethan pulpit and a vast organ built in 1893.' In 1741, the spire was blown down and rebuilt in 1748. A second rebuilding took place in 1879 - this is the spire in the photograph. On 23 March 1918, an aircraft from the RAF (previously the RFC) station at Wyton landed in a nearby water meadow for the pilot ask some local lads the way back to the airfield. Shortly after taking off, the aircraft veered sharply and clipped the top thirty or so feet from the top of the spire - the pilot was killed instantly. A section of the spire was renewed in 1924.

ST IVES
The Broadway 1898 41278

This photograph was taken from where the memorial commemorating the Diamond Jubilee of Queen Victoria's accession now stands. It was to be unveiled on 26 June 1902 - the proposed date for King Edward VII's coronation - but his illness delayed the ceremony. Unfortunately, the memorial had already been carved and the stone laid - so the date remains. Today, in the premises occupied by C F Clarke, jeweller and furniture dealer (right), the Local Cafe and St Ives Fried Chicken provide lunchtime snacks for the people working in the town. Next door are B R Jones, photographer, and Vesuvio Pizza. The wooden structure outside Mr Clarke's shop is designed to support the awning for his sun blinds.

ST IVES, *The Broadway 1901* 48071

It is three years after No 41278, and little has changed; the memorial is still a year away. On the left is the North Hunts Constitutional Club, now the offices of Ewing Reeson, photographer. The young child on the tricycle rides past the Unicorn, now the premises of Wadsworth's, the beer, wine and spirit merchants, who have moved from their office on Bridge Street. Then comes a fish and chip shop, an Indian take-away and the apparently closed E H Deer, a tobacco and newsagent's. In the distance, we can see the original buildings between Crown Street and the old Merry Lane. The Broadway was the site of the original market: the area on the far left was known as Baker's Row, to the near left was the Bullock Market, and on the right was Tanners' Row. The market was closed in October 1886 and trade moved to join the Sheep Market, which was already well established in Market Hill.

ST IVES, *Crown Street 1925* 77198

Crown Street connects the Bullock Market and Market Hill. It takes its name from the Crown public house (right) opposite the turning to Bridge Street, now occupied by Woolworth's. Next door, with the two gabled doorways, stands the post office, built in 1887 on the site of the Old Court House. It was totally demolished in 1986 and rebuilt in a sympathetic style - it incorporates some of the original features, including the carved plaque in the roof apex. It is now occupied by a branch of Superdrug. Barclays Bank on the extreme right was built in the early 19th century. It is now owned by Dewhurst the butcher, and apart from a rather more modern frontage, survives intact.

ST IVES
The Sheep Market,
Market Hill 1931 84547

All of the sheep pens have now disappeared, and the cobbled section of the Sheep Market has been built over. A paved pedestrian area covers the pens, and today traders of all kinds sell their goods from colourful stalls at the busy Monday Market. In the background the silhouette of the row of shops has hardly changed. From left to right, we can see W Golding & Son, hardware; The Ivo Café; Rowells, tailors and outfitters; The Old Robin Hood public house; and Radfords, an upholsterer. In the distance stands Rustons the ironmonger's, whilst on the right is the White Hart public house and Dilley (later Ekins, Dilley & Handley), auctioneers. Standing proudly above them all is the spire of the Free Church.

ST IVES, *Oliver Cromwell's Statue, Market Hill 1901* 48069

Shortly before this photograph was taken, the Town Council approved an expenditure of £850 to be paid to Frederick Pomeroy RA for the design and execution of a statue of the Lord Protector. It had originally been envisaged that it should stand in Huntingdon, but the town had always had Royalist inclinations and there was little interest from the people. Cromwell had lived at St Ives from 1631 to 1635, and the townsfolk took the project to heart. The globes in the photograph were made of copper, and were part of the original design. They were removed in the 1970s and never replaced. Today, cast iron replicas adorn the pedestals.

▶ **ST IVES**
Market Hill c1950 S23008

On non-market days, the centre of St Ives was a quiet and unhurried place. There are few cars other than those parked between the Cromwell statue and the war memorial, and people are able to pass the time of day in the middle of the road. J W Angood, the cycle and motor-cycle repairer (right), seems to have been busy: seven or eight of his customer's machines await collection. Before he took over, the shop had been owned by Rowell & Sons, tailors. Next door is Senescall's animal and petfood store - today the site is occupied by a Help the Aged shop.

ST IVES
Market Hill c1955
S23030

By 1955, Market Hill has become a little busier. If we look northwards towards Crown Street along what is now called The Pavement, we see that the frontages of the shops have changed little over the past fifty or so years, although many of the old St Ives names have gone. The shops behind the 'sit up and beg' Ford and the Sunbeam Talbot 90 are occupied by Barnardos and Taylor's the estate agents, while the whole of Fosters, outfitters, and the shop next door are taken up by Mackays. The building hidden behind Cromwell is now held by Thompson Morris, the estate agents, and to its left, Robert Kiddle & Son, furnishers and removals and the taxi office have been taken by Choices.

ST IVES, *The Square c1965* S23105

ST IVES
Market Day 1931 84549

In 1931, there seems to be very little trade at the market around the war memorial and outside the Golden Lion (to the left of the church). Maybe the stalls are setting up or possibly closing down for the day? The Golden Lion rose in importance with the coaching business and, consequently, trade at the Crown dwindled. With the arrival of the railway, the Golden Lion offered its horse-drawn omnibus to meet travellers at the station. By the 1870s, the Great Northern Railway had its own office at the premises. The war memorial was erected in 1921 to remember those who fell in the Great War. A number of names had to be added after he Second World War. By 1965, the market stalls have moved across the road, and the old site has been taken over by parked cars. It was in front of the Free Church that a great town feast took place to celebrate the coronation of George V in 1911. Twenty long trestle tables, each seating about forty people, were ranged across Market Hill, and the buildings were decked with flags, bunting and patriotic slogans. The Free Church was built in 1864-65 to house the congregations of the former Independent and Baptist Chapels. The town's tradition of nonconformity dates back to the time of Oliver Cromwell. With the joining of the Primitive Methodists in 1971, the Free Church became the United Reformed Church. It is interesting to compare the spires of the Free Church and the Parish Church. That on the Free Church is five feet higher - it would have brought a smile to Cromwell's face!

HOUSE FURNISHER &c

H. RADFORD

▼ **HOUGHTON,** *The Mill 1899* 44258

The mill at Houghton was owned by Potto Brown. He is remembered in the village for his entrepreneurial and philanthropic activities. He provided a fine school for the children, and arranged that allotments should be provided for all the village men. A staunch non-conformist, Potto Brown lies buried at Houghton Chapel; it is said that he took his accounting books there to enlist God's help in making sure that those who owed him money paid their bills. A mill has been recorded at Houghton since AD974, and this building continued to grind corn until 1930. Today, the mill is owned and operated by the National Trust and is open to the public.

► **HOUGHTON**
The Mill House and the Church 1898 41292

Opposite the lock on the Great Ouse stands the Mill House. This fine Victorian building with its intricate diaper brickwork was the home of the miller; the owner of the mill, Potto Brown, lived in a far grander house in the village. The brick and stone landing stage is protected by large baulks of timber to prevent damage to the barges which carried produce along the river and the ferry boat taking passengers and goods across to the Hemingfords.

◄ HOUGHTON
The Village 1914 66963

The name Houghton, always pronounced 'Hoe'ton', has its origins in Saxon times, although there is evidence that there was a settlement here before the Roman period. The village, with its partner Wyton, developed along the road leading from Huntingdon to St Ives. Running parallel to the south of the road, the Great Ouse meanders between the two towns, and Houghton took advantage of both road and waterborne trade. Today, the roads are busy and congested, whilst the river continues on its silent way, witnessing only the occasional pleasure craft. Houghton was the home of the artists William Watt Milne, 1865-1949, and Charles Whymper, 1853-1941. The latter was the brother of Edward Whymper, who was the first person to climb the Matterhorn.

► HOUGHTON
The Clock Tower c1960
H464008

This is probably one of the most photographed views in Huntingdonshire. The thatched clock tower at Houghton was erected in 1902 as a memorial to Potto Brown's son, George. It has two clock faces: neither are visible in the photograph, as they both face in the opposite direction! Around the tower is parked a group of typical 1960s cars - two Morris Minors (a Traveller and a saloon), a Mini-van, a Morris Oxford Farina and a Standard Pennant. There can be little doubt regarding the date.

▶ **HOUGHTON**
St Ives Road c1960
H464006

These are the first cottages that the visitor entering the village from the north will see. Nothing has changed since 1960; the road curves gently past these unspoilt 16th-century timber-framed buildings. The jettied house in the centre of the view, adjacent to The Lanes, has '1590' above the door, and there is little evidence to dispute this date. The thatched cottage just visible on the left is called May Cottage - a popular name in the locality! Traffic today is a little busier, and just out of the picture is the workshop of Beers, motor engineers, well known for their preparation of racing and rallying MG cars. The lady on her bicycle might be advised to keep closer to the pavement!

◀ **HARTFORD**
The Parish Church of All Saints' 1898 41261

Hartford is now an eastern suburb of Huntingdon and Godmanchester. It lies astride the main road between Huntingdon and St Ives and along the course of the Great Ouse. All Saints' stands close to the river, and is protected from the scouring effect of the Ouse by a low wall which encloses a small but immaculately maintained churchyard. On the landward side of the church there is a second well-kept overspill graveyard, where a new meeting hall with kitchens and toilets is presently being built. The Hollow leads from the landing stage adjacent to the church northwards towards the main village of Hartford.

▲ **HARTFORD,** *The Village 1907* 58554

Moving northwards from the church along the Hollow, the path crosses Main Street into Sapley Road. It is difficult today to imagine that this is the sight that would have greeted travellers. The house on the left has been totally restored and renovated. The building opposite has changed beyond description. Only the Barley Mow (ahead), built using the stone from the spire of St Benedict's Church at Huntingdon, survives; it is now a bustling and busy roadhouse full of the sound of piped music and merry chatter. One wonders what Henry Stevens, the landlord in 1907, would have thought of the modern Barley Mow - and we might ask why he decided to sport a White Ensign endorsed 'The People' on the front wall of the pub.

◀ **ABBOTS RIPTON**
The Flower Garden
c1955 A304003

The parish of Abbots Ripton lies a few miles north of Huntingdon. At the time of the Dissolution it was held by Ramsey Abbey. The village was called Ripton until it was owned by the abbey, when and the forename 'Abbots' was added. The main wealth of the parish lay in the high quality of the soil and the extensive woodland. This flower garden, with its grass walks and sundials, flourishes in the best soil in the neighbourhood.

69

▼ **BRAMPTON PARK** *1898* 41264

Brampton Park covers about 100 acres and in 1898 it was the property of the Duke of
Manchester. There had been a grand house on the site since the 12th century. By 1328,
the original building was in a ruinous state, and later a new house was built by the
Throckmorton family. Around 1820, the house was rebuilt by Lady Olivia Bernard Sparrow.
In 1889 this became an 'Institute for the cure of stammerers.' In 1907 a spectacular fire
destroyed the building, and a replacement was built for Viscount Mandeville.

▶ **BRAMPTON**
The Village 1907 58560

Honeypot Cottage, in the centre of the village,
is said once to have been a hospital. Today it
is almost totally obscured by trees and shrubs,
and you could be forgiven for missing it. The
photograph was taken from the site of the village
sign which was erected in 1988 to commemorate
the 70th anniversary of the founding of the
village's Women's Institute. The house in the
centre with the white barge boards has been
demolished, and in its place is one of those self-
cleaning public conveniences and a row of shops
containing a pharmacy and a dental surgery. On
the opposite side, the Horse Shoe has changed
into the friendly Brampton Fish Bar - a welcome
facility in this village on a cold day. Just out of the
picture, behind the photographer and marking
the focal point of the community, stands the base
of the village's 14th-century market cross.

◄ BRAMPTON
The Green 1955 B182013

It was at Brampton that John Pepys, father of Samuel Pepys the diarist, inherited a large property worth about £80 per year. It is said that an iron pot full of silver coins found at the foot of a wall in 1842 was part of a cache hidden by Samuel Pepys during the Great Plague. This view showing the now disappeared telephone kiosk was taken from the spot where forty years later the Rt Honourable John Major, a local resident, planted an oak tree to commemorate 100 years of the Brampton Parish Council. Peeping under the trees on the right is the Methodist church built in 1889. The grass in the foreground awaits the attention of a lawn mower - today, it would not need to wait, as Brampton prides itself for its regular success in the Huntingdonshire 'Best Kept Village' competition.

► BRAMPTON
The Royal Oak and the Signpost c1955 B182016

A few hundred yards along the present B1514 road past the turning to Pepys House, the road forks at the roundabout where the main road runs eastwards towards the A14 and the left road takes us into the village of Brampton. Up to the 1970s, the Royal Oak public house offered a welcome break to travellers before they moved on to London or Thrapston. Today there is no sign of the pub, and only a housing estate marks the spot. The obelisk-like signpost, however, survives on the entry to a roundabout. Carved hands tells the correct road to take, but they could be missed if the driver chose that moment to blink.

71

▼ **BRAMPTON,** *The High Street c1955* B182015

In the last forty or so years, very little has changed in the High Street, although the recently built premises of the Midland Bank (right) has now become a private house. The Community Centre still provides all kinds of activities from its fine white building beyond, which today sports a group of plaques won in the Huntingdon 'Best Kept Village' competition. On the opposite of the road to the thatched Three Chimneys next door are Falcon Cottage, White Doves bed & breakfast and the recently built Bonnetts Flour Sac. The latter is a branch of Bonnetts, who were originally founded around 1804.

► **GODMANCHESTER**
The Chinese Bridge
c1955 G24043

The town's impressive Chinese Bridge was built in 1827 - the name reflects the design of the bridge. It links Post Street to the riverside walk on the west side of the Ouse. At this point, the river is placid, and silver fish can be seen darting just below the surface; to the south, in the still water by the Causeway, all kinds of ducks and wading birds are fed by the visiting children.

◀ **GODMANCHESTER**
The Ouse from the Old Mill 1898 41271

We are looking southwards onto the Ouse from the site of the Old Mill. The houses and shops along the causeway are visible behind the Chinese Bridge. Many of the properties backing onto the river had their own boathouses and landing stages, and one rowing boat is moored against the bank. Today, the bank is lined with brick summerhouses and gazebos, whilst the opposite bank forms a pretty riverside walk.

▶ **GODMANCHESTER**
The Bridge 1901 46625

This photograph looks northwards along the Ouse from the riverside walk. The footpath crosses the river firstly over the weir and then across the Chinese Bridge. The building with the bell tower below the church is the old Grammar School founded in 1559, although mostly rebuilt in the mid 19th century. The plaque on its wall records its foundation and subsequent restoration in 1851 and 1987: it reads 'Eliz reg hujus scholae fundatrix' ('Queen Elizabeth founded this school'). To the left of the school are the Council Offices, which were restored in 1979.

73

► **GODMANCHESTER**
The Causeway c1955
G24016

The shops along the Causeway, facing the Ouse basin, have changed very little. Townsend's Stores (left) have become J G Clifford, dispensing chemist; the tearooms and cafe are now Riverside Hair Design; Ali's Tandoori Restaurant lies on the opposite side of the arched gateway. The bay windowed building is Hampton House, whilst the Royal Oak, on the other side of St Ann's Lane, continues to provide refreshment to the boating fraternity.

◄ **GODMANCHESTER**
The Causeway 1929 81882

While the village lads pose for the camera and the girls stroll nonchalantly by on the other side, a 'bullnose' Morris overtakes a horse and cart. The jettied, gabled building (centre right) was renovated in the early 1950s and is home to the Riverside Fish and Chip Shop. The next part of the half-timbered complex is still a chemist and optician's practice - today John & Doris Clifford. The building closest to the camera has changed little, but it underwent extensive restoration and cleaning during the spring of 2004.

▲ **GODMANCHESTER,** *The Causeway c1955* G24042

This is almost the same view as 81882, but twenty-five years later. The bullnose Morris has been replaced by a Chevrolet Corvair, whilst a Hillman Minx is parked outside the opticians. The landing stage has become a little derelict and overgrown. By 2004, it had all but disappeared, but the Causeway is unchanged.

◄ **GODMANCHESTER**
The Church of St Mary the Virgin
1898 41274

Photographed from the north-east when the lands to the north were under water, the church is silhouetted against the sky. The church was built between 1623 and 1625 of materials from the original 13th-century structure. The cost of erecting the tower and spire were funded by public subscription - those who failed to pay went to prison. Today, the wet land has been drained and forms part of the school playing field, and the rather unkempt burial ground is a haven for butterflies and all kinds of wildlife. Inside the gate leading to Church Place are memorials to the Hunnybun family; a branch of this family were well-known coach builders and harness makers in Cambridge.

GODMANCHESTER
Cambridge Street
1929 81883

The main road leading from Godmanchester to Cambridge and St Ives has changed little in appearance, although redevelopment makes the exact location of this view impossible to identify. The road has been widened, and many of the houses have been rebuilt in a style similar to that of the mid1800s. However, the couple of motor-cars would be swamped by the busy nose-to-tail rush hour traffic today.

HUNTINGDON, *Hinchingbrook House 1907* 58552

The house was built around the remains of a former Benedictine nunnery. At the time of the Dissolution, Sir Richard Cromwell was given the estate by Henry VIII; it is said that as a child, Oliver Cromwell played here. Later, Hinchingbrook was taken by the Montagu, family who became the Earls of Sandwich (it was from one of the earls that the sandwich snack took its name). Hinchingbrook House is now home to the Sixth Form Centre of Hinchingbrook School, and is open to the public every Sunday afternoon in the summer.

HUNTINGDON
Delivery to the International Stores, High Street c1955
H136019V

Close to the corner of Grammar School Walk and the High Street, a
Morris Commercial lorry belonging to SPD delivers a consignment to
the International Stores. The premises had once been the town's post
office, and is today occupied by Savers film processing shop.

◄ HUNTINGDON
The George Hotel Yard c1960 H136040

With the decline of the coaching trade, the proprietors of the George sought other sources of income. The arrival of the railway improved business a little, but it was the newfangled motor car which saw a return to prosperity. The George advertised that it could provide accommodation for 100 cars!

HUNTINGDON, *North End 1906* 55424x

◄ HUNTINGDON, *North End 1906* 55424

The view shows the Rose and Crown public house and, on the right, the row of fine mansard roofed terraced houses. Each of the doorways has its own fine web fanlight. It was close to here that Charles Windover had his coachworks, where he built car bodies for Rolls-Royce, amongst others. Amongst their most successful bodies was the Marlborough limousine constructed on the Renault chassis. The works moved to London in the early 1930s.

▶ **HUNTINGDON**
The High Street looking West
1906 55420x

▼ **HUNTINGDON**
The High Street looking West
1929 81876

Only the motor-car and the lady
polishing the window of Smith's bread
shop (left, 81876 below) give away
the different dates of these views.
On the right, the railings of St Mary's
churchyard lead down to the Bull and
the vicarage, which was demolished to
make way for the widening of Hartford
Street. Dominating the skyline is the
elegant spire of Trinity Church, which
was taken down in the 1960s as part of
the town centre 'improvement' plan.
The shop fronts and premises along
the High Street have now all been
modernized, and what had changed
little in the time between these
photographs were taken is now barely
recognisable.

HUNTINGDON
The Montagu Club, Hartford Road 1906
55423 (detail of a larger picture)

In 1897, the 8th Earl of Sandwich endowed the Montagu Club for education and recreation purposes. It is of fine red and yellow brick set against black banding. The iron railings and pillars were removed during the Second World War, and the space behind them is now used for parking. Above the door are two plaques, one bearing the date 1897 and the other depicting the arms of the Sandwich/ Montagu family.

HUNTINGDON, *All Saints' Church from Market Hill 1960* H130043

In 1906, the Frith photographer stood at exactly the same spot and photographed All Saints'. Coming back just over fifty years later, he would have recognised the view, for little has changed. Only the notice board and the bench are new, although the railings, like so many others, had been removed as part of the war effort. Today, the railings have been replaced, and each of the wrought iron spear heads depicts one of the leaves that can be found on the trees in the churchyard and surrounding area. Among the treasures of the church is the font from St John's church in which, it is said, Oliver Cromwell was baptized.

HUNTINGDON, *The High Street looking East 1955* H136003

In the foreground on the left is the Huntingdon Co-operative store, but overshadowing the whole of the street is the spire of Trinity Church. This was a bold statement of the strength of non-conformity in the town; at 182 feet, it outshone the seemingly insignificant towers of the parish churches. Trinity Church was built in 1867-68 for the Baptists and the Congregationalists, and Potto Brown of Houghton contributed £12,000 towards the cost. The planners of the new town centre had no place in their design for this beautiful building, and it was swept away in 1965-66 and replaced by a branch of Tesco. A new Trinity Free Church was built in Buttsgrove Way.

◄ **HUNTINGDON**
The Cromwell Museum c1960 H136042

▼ **HUNTINGDON**
Cromwell's Grammar School 1929 81880

The sole museum celebrating the life and work of Oliver Cromwell is housed in the Old Grammar School at Huntingdon. The museum was opened in 1961, and has undergone extensive reconstruction and renovation in 2004. It contains an impressive collection and display of memorabilia relating to the Lord Protector. As well as Cromwell, Samuel Pepys was a pupil in the Grammar School.

▶ HUNTINGDON
Market Hill 1929 81874

Today Market Hill has been pedestrianised, and it makes a pleasant and tranquil area to walk and rest from the noise of traffic. In 1929, a few cars including a bullnose Morris Cowley and a Vauxhall 14 wait to be collected by their owners. Even if you could gain access to the Hill today, it would be unthinkable to leave your car, maybe the equivalent of the Morris 10, with its roof down - apart from car alarms and sophisticated locking devices, the square is surveyed by a closed circuit TV system! On the left is Wykeham House, once the Westminster Bank, now home to the town's Register Office, whilst behind it is the County Careers Guidance Office. The war memorial is known as the Thinking Soldier, and was designed by Lady Kathleen Scott, widow of Scott of the Antarctic. The soldier, who looks eastwards towards France, stands on an engraved stone plinth which not only remembers those who served in the two world wars but also 'those in the many wars and conflicts since 1945 [who] served and died to preserve freedom.'

◀ HUNTINGDON
St Mary's Church c1965 H136070

This is one of the few Huntingdon churches which survived the turmoil of the Civil War and the 20th-century programme of 'civic improvement.' In 1428 it was badly damaged by fire and had to be rebuilt. During 1607, the tower fell away from the western wall and collapsed into the nave; again, it was rebuilt. Further major restorations were carried out during 1876 when the roof and eastern wall were replaced.

▲ **HUNTINGDON,** *The Old Bridge 1898* 41251

▼ **HUNTINGDON,** *The Old Bridge 1929* 81873

The bridge has hardly changed during the thirty years that separate our photographs. Until the construction of the A14 bypass, visitors to the town entered via he Old North Road through this narrow medieval bridge and into the busy High Street. The stone, six-arched bridge was built in 1332, and was only superseded in 1975 when the new bypass flyover was built.

HUNTINGDON
The Bridge and the River from Castle Hill c1955 H136008

Around 1855, Charles Veasey built a steam-powered mill manufacturing linseed oil and cattle cake. The mill, on the south bank of the Great Ouse, later became a hosiery factory, and has now been converted into a prestige housing complex. In the background stands the flour mill of Brown & Goodman. This was built in 1861 and contained sixteen pairs of grinding stones; it was demolished in 1969. The photograph was taken from Castle Hill, the site of the castle, which was built in 1068 and destroyed by Henry II in 1173. Nothing survives other than a grassy mound.

HUNTINGDON, *The Hospital and the Fountain 1906* 55420a

The hospital was opened in 1854 by Edward Fellowes, MP. There were two wards each for men and women with a total of 26 beds. The hospital was extended in 1864 and 1897, and the Edward VII Memorial Ward was added in 1912. The terracotta fountain was built in 1889 to commemorate the late 7th Earl of Sandwich, but by the early 1980s it had deteriorated to such an extent that it had to be removed.

INDEX

NAMES OF SUBSCRIBERS

The following people have kindly supported this book by subscribing to copies before publication.

In Memory of Annie Anderson

Mrs D. S. Banyard

Mrs H. Booth

Mr G. & Mrs M. Booth, St Neots

The People of Brampton, Huntingdonshire

Victor W. Bridges, St Ives

Mr A. E. G. & Mrs Y. A. Buckle, Canvey Island

Heather Bunyan-Smith, St Neots

Glenda Diane Burden

In Memory of Grandad Burden

Bob Burn-Murdoch, Norris Museum, St Ives

As a tribute to my Parents. Alan Carter

Roger & Philippa Clode, Fowey

Danielle, Zoe and Ben

Malcolm Fletcher, Godmanchester

Isobel & Geoffrey Frost May 2004

Jeanette Hannah George

C. M. Goscomb, St Ives

R. Goscomb, St Ives

The Hardy Family, Godmanchester

Mr D. C. Hufford

Huntingdon, St Neots and St Ives Town Crier Series

Pauline & Brian Jones

Mr K. R. Lewington, London

Mr D. & Mrs E. L. Liddle

Larry & Katie Mann, St Ives

Mrs Valerie Miles and sons Richard & Russell

Christine Mockford

The Montague Family, St Neots

Debbie S. Moss, St Ives, Cambs

Happy Anniversary Mum and Dad from Julia

Dick & Jenny Newman
and Mrs Doris Newman 93 yrs

The Nicholas Rebane Family, Cambridge

Bev Nicoliades, Hilton

Armando Nigro

The Old School House, Hemingford Abbots

To Aunty Olwen love Glenda

Beryl Parsons

M. J. Peak & L. Peak, St Ives

Kerry Pearce & Corrinne Nisbet 2004

St Neots Picture Gallery, Eynesbury

Morning Coffee Staff at St Neots U R Church

Julien Saker 8th October 2004

In Memory of Wendy N. Saker, St Ives

Mr J. W. & Mrs V. A Smoothy, St Ives, Cambs

Frederick S. Swaine, Huntingdon

Taggert Gallery and Tile Museum,
Great Staughton

To Vivien on your birthday

The Ward Family, Godmanchester

In Memory of Mr & Mrs S. A. Ward, Fenstanton

In Memory of Robert & Mary Ann Wheal

FRITH PRODUCTS & SERVICES

Francis Frith would doubtless be pleased to know that the pioneering publishing venture he started in 1860 still continues today. Over a hundred and forty years later, The Francis Frith Collection continues in the same innovative tradition and is now one of the foremost publishers of vintage photographs in the world. Some of the current activities include:

INTERIOR DECORATION

Today Frith's photographs can be seen framed and as giant wall murals in thousands of pubs, restaurants, hotels, banks, retail stores and other public buildings throughout the country. In every case they enhance the unique local atmosphere of the places they depict and provide reminders of gentler days in an increasingly busy and frenetic world.

PRODUCT PROMOTIONS

Frith products are used by many major companies to promote the sales of their own products or to reinforce their own history and heritage. Frith promotions have been used by Hovis bread, Courage beers, Scots Porage Oats, Colman's mustard, Cadbury's foods, Mellow Birds coffee, Dunhill pipe tobacco, Guinness, and Bulmer's Cider.

GENEALOGY AND FAMILY HISTORY

As the interest in family history and roots grows world-wide, more and more people are turning to Frith's photographs of Great Britain for images of the towns, villages and streets where their ancestors lived; and, of course, photographs of the churches and chapels where their ancestors were christened, married and buried are an essential part of every genealogy tree and family album.

FRITH PRODUCTS

All Frith photographs are available Framed or just as Mounted Prints and Posters (size 23 x 16 inches). These may be ordered from the address below. Other products available are - Address Books, Calendars, Jigsaws, Canvas Prints, Postcards and local and prestige books.

THE INTERNET

Already ninety thousand Frith photographs can be viewed and purchased on the internet through the Frith websites and a myriad of partner sites.

For more detailed information on Frith products, look at this site:
www.francisfrith.com

See the complete list of Frith Books at: www.francisfrith.com
This web site is regularly updated with the latest list of publications from The Francis Frith Collection. If you wish to buy books relating to another part of the country that your local bookshop does not stock, you may purchase on-line.

For further information, trade, or author enquiries please contact us at the address below:
The Francis Frith Collection, 6 Oakley Business Park, Wylye Road, Dinton, Wiltshire SP3 5EU.
Tel: +44 (0)1722 716 376 Fax: +44 (0)1722 716 881 Email: sales@francisfrith.co.uk

---

See Frith products on the internet at www.francisfrith.com

FREE PRINT OF YOUR CHOICE
CHOOSE A PHOTOGRAPH FROM THIS BOOK
+ £3.80 POSTAGE

Mounted Print
Overall size 14 x 11 inches (355 x 280mm)

TO RECEIVE YOUR FREE PRINT

Choose any Frith photograph in this book

Simply complete the Voucher opposite and
return it with your remittance for £3.80 (to cover
postage and handling) and we will print the
photograph of your choice in SEPIA (size 11 x 8
inches) and supply it in a cream mount ready to
frame (overall size 14 x 11 inches).

Order additional Mounted Prints
at HALF PRICE - £12.00 each (normally £24.00)

If you would like to order more Frith prints
from this book, possibly as gifts for friends and
family, you can buy them at half price (with no
additional postage costs).

Have your Mounted Prints framed

For an extra £20.00 per print you can have your
mounted print(s) framed in an elegant polished
wood and gilt moulding, overall size
16 x 13 inches (no additional postage required).

IMPORTANT!

❶ Please note: aerial photographs and photographs
with a reference number starting with a "Z" are not Frith
photographs and cannot be supplied under this offer.

❷ Offer valid for delivery to one UK address only.

❸ These special prices are only available if you use this
form to order. You must use the ORIGINAL VOUCHER on
this page (no copies permitted). We can only despatch
to one UK address.

❹ This offer cannot be combined with any other offer.

As a customer your name & address will be stored by Frith but not sold or rented
to third parties. Your data will be used for the purpose of this promotion only.

Send completed Voucher form to:

The Francis Frith Collection,
6 Oakley Business Park, Wylie Road,
Dinton, Wiltshire SP3 5EU

Voucher for **FREE**
and *Reduced Price*
Frith Prints

*Please do not photocopy this voucher. Only the original is valid,
so please fill it in, cut it out and return it to us with your order.*

Picture ref no	Page no	Qty	Mounted @ £12.00	Framed + £20.00	Total Cost £
		1	Free of charge*	£	£
			£12.00	£	£
			£12.00	£	£
			£12.00	£	£
			£12.00	£	£
			£12.00	£	£

*Please allow 28 days
for delivery.
Offer available to one
UK address only*

* Post & handling		£3.80
Total Order Cost		**£**

Title of this book . . . .

I enclose a cheque/postal order for £ . . . .
made payable to 'The Francis Frith Collection'

OR please debit my Mastercard / Visa / Maestro card,
details below

Card Number:

Issue No (Maestro only):   Valid from (Maestro):

Card Security Number: Expires:

Signature:

Name Mr/Mrs/Ms . . . .

Address . . . .

. . . .

. . . .

. . . . Postcode . . . .

Daytime Tel No . . . .

Email . . . .

Valid to 31/12/15

Free Print – see overleaf

Can you help us with information about any of the Frith photographs in this book?

We are gradually compiling an historical record for each of the photographs in the Frith archive. It is always fascinating to find out the names of the people shown in the pictures, as well as insights into the shops, buildings and other features depicted.

If you recognize anyone in the photographs in this book, or if you have information not already included in the author's caption, do let us know. We would love to hear from you, and will try to publish it in future books or articles.

An Invitation from The Francis Frith Collection to Share Your Memories

The 'Share Your Memories' feature of our website allows members of the public to add personal memories relating to the places featured in our photographs, or comment on others already added. Seeing a place from your past can rekindle forgotten or long held memories. Why not visit the website, find photographs of places you know well and add YOUR story for others to read and enjoy? We would love to hear from you!

www.francisfrith.com/memories

Our production team

Frith books are produced by a small dedicated team at offices near Salisbury. Most have worked with the Frith Collection for many years. All have in common one quality: they have a passion for the Frith Collection.

Frith Books and Gifts

We have a wide range of books and gifts available on our website utilising our photographic archive, many of which can be individually personalised.

www.francisfrith.com

Contains material sourced from responsibly managed forests.

FF012143